BOOBIES

by Nancy Vo

Groundwood Books
House of Anansi Press
Toronto / Berkeley

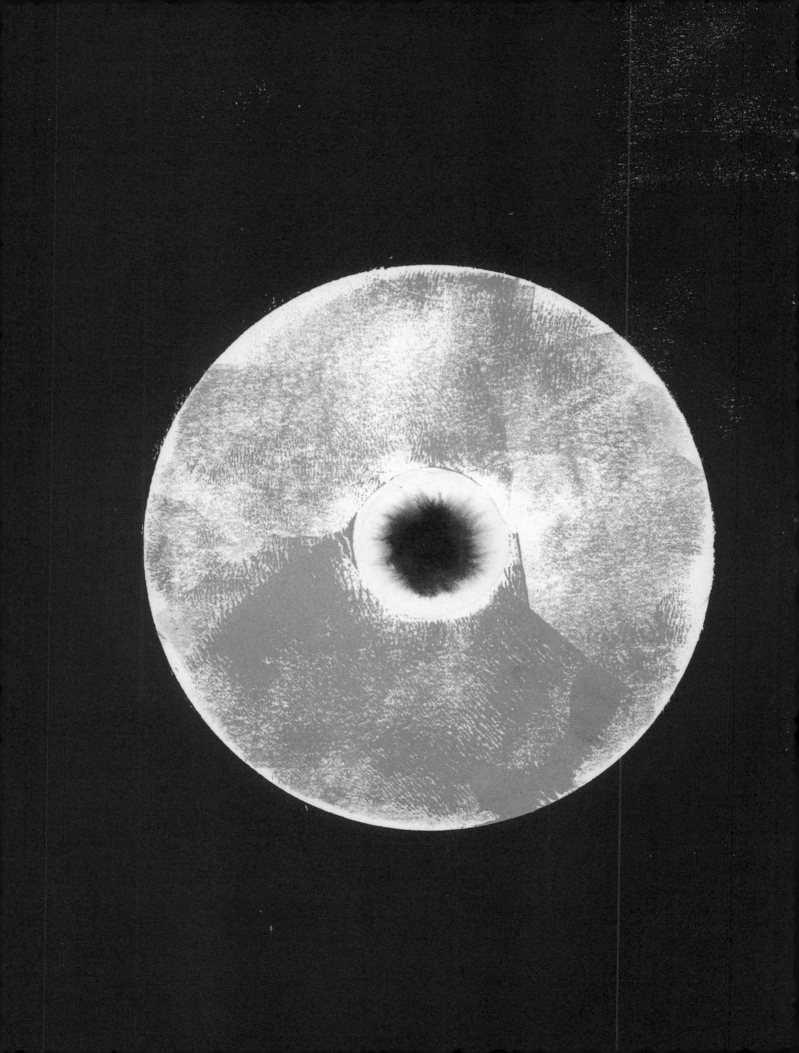

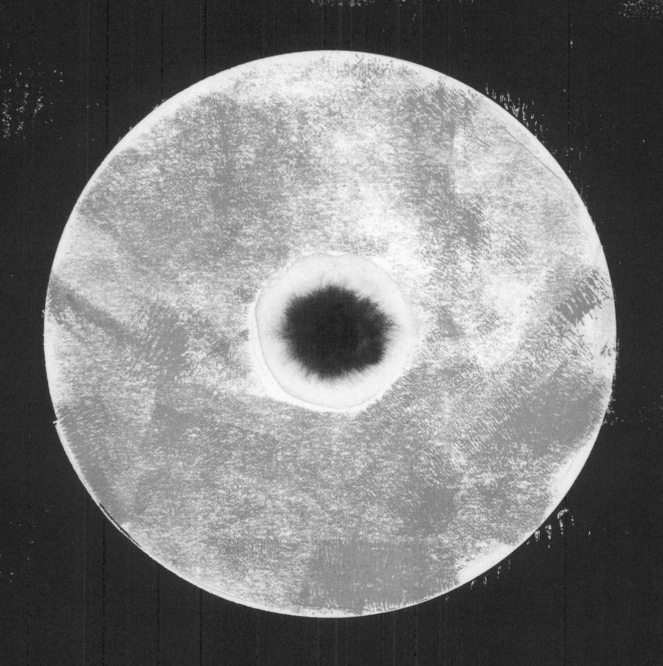

You have just opened a
book about boobies.

Here is a Blue-footed Booby.

But wait … the Blue-footed Booby does
not have any boobies at all.

Birds are avian, not mammalian.
Mammals have mammary glands.
In other words, mammals have boobies.

Look!
Which of these animals have boobies?

A dog?
Yes.

A cat?
Yes.

A hamster?
Yes.

A fish?
No. Fish are not mammals.

You?
Yes, you are a mammal too.
You are a human mammal.

Just as humans
vary, boobies vary.

Not only that,
your boobies will
change as you
grow up and as
you grow older.

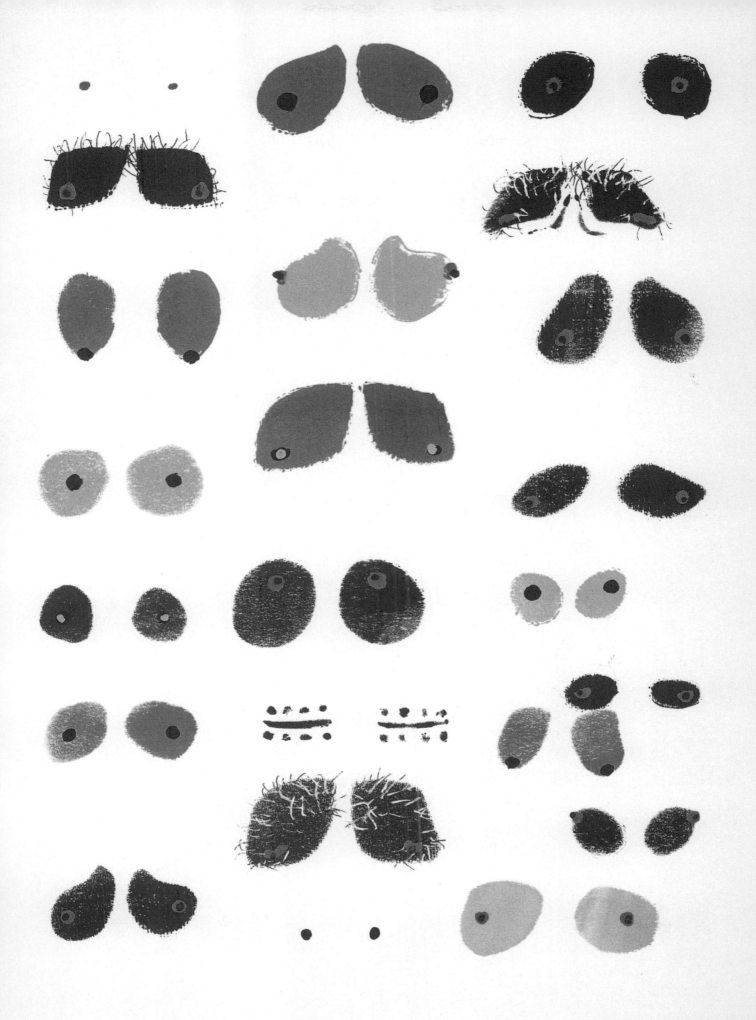

You may wonder, why do we have boobies?

The mammary glands in boobies can make milk to feed babies.

Human boobies are called breasts, so we call this breastfeeding.

But not all milk comes from mammals.

Some humans like to milk plants.

Look! This new mama dog has ten boobies. But the number of boobies is not the same as the number of puppies she can have at once.

How many puppies do you see?

Do different kinds of mammals have different numbers of boobies?
Yes.

Cats have six to eight boobies.

Rats have twelve boobies.

Pigs have twelve to fourteen boobies.

Humans only have two boobies.

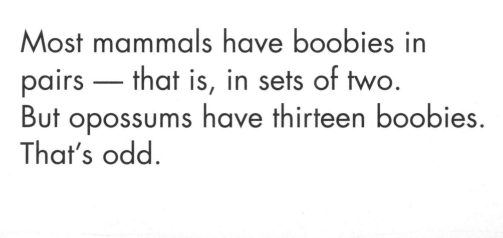

Most mammals have boobies in pairs — that is, in sets of two. But opossums have thirteen boobies. That's odd.

A cow's mammary glands are in a bowl shape, with four booby tubes.
Udderly fascinating!

Mammal boobies can protrude, especially when they make milk.
Protrude like mountains, hills and molehills.
This must be uncomfortable for our shorter four-legged friends.

There are
mountains that
some say are
named after
boobies.

Three of them.
"Les Trois Tétons."

The tallest is called
Grand Teton.

ROCKY MOUNTAINS, USA

Yellowstone
National
Park

Grand Teton
National
Park

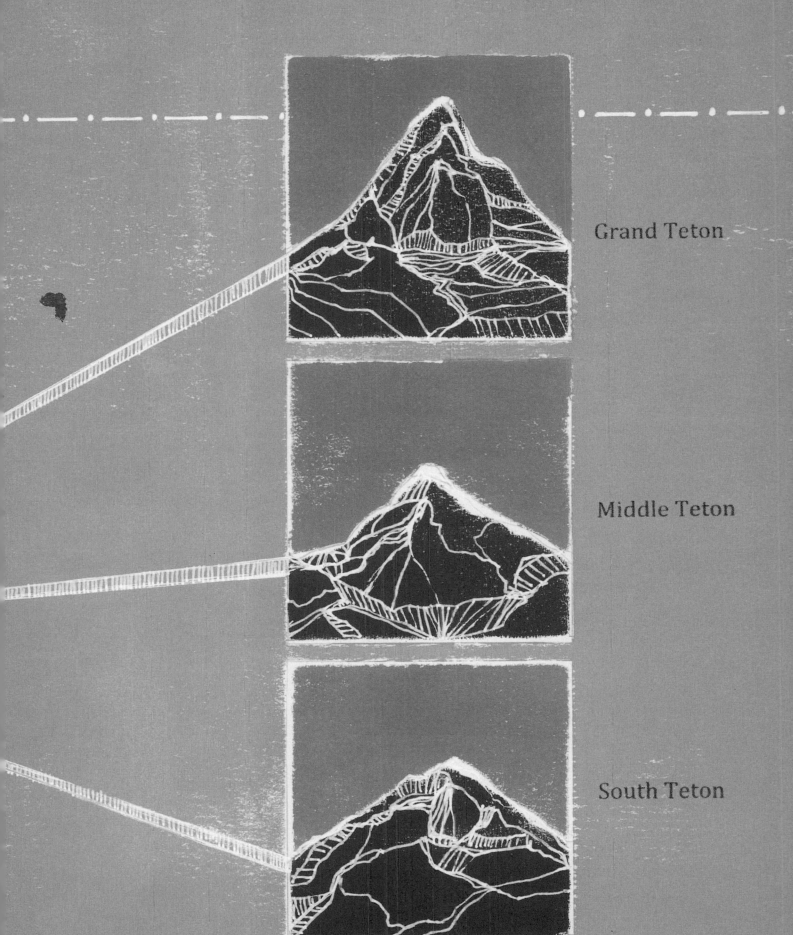

Grand Teton

Middle Teton

South Teton

And did you know that "mountain peaks" is Chinese slang for boobies?

Look!
Humans have carved
boobies out of stone
and wood for more
than 25,000 years.

Boobiologists know
that boobies have been
around and round for
a long time.

So don't be shy.
Say it like you
mean it ...

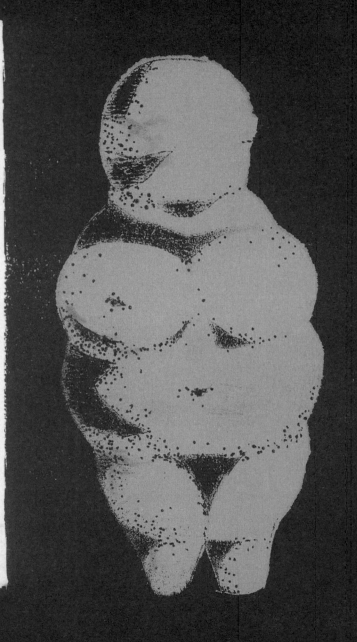

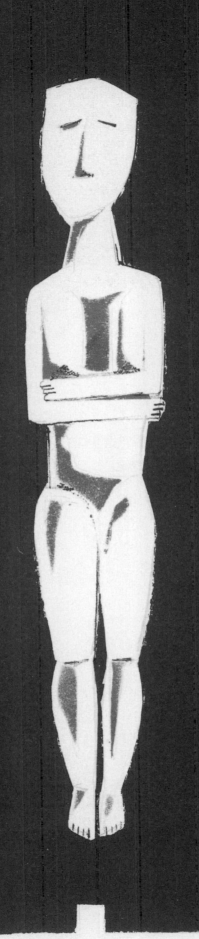

2500 BCE   1900 CE

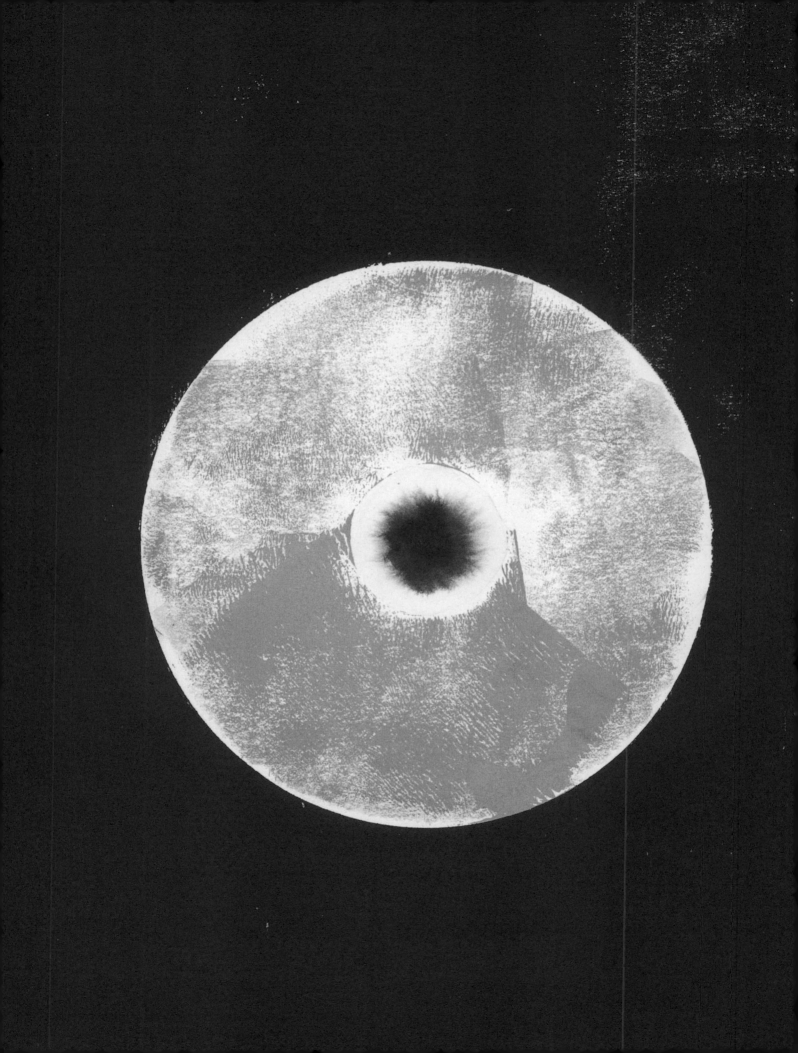

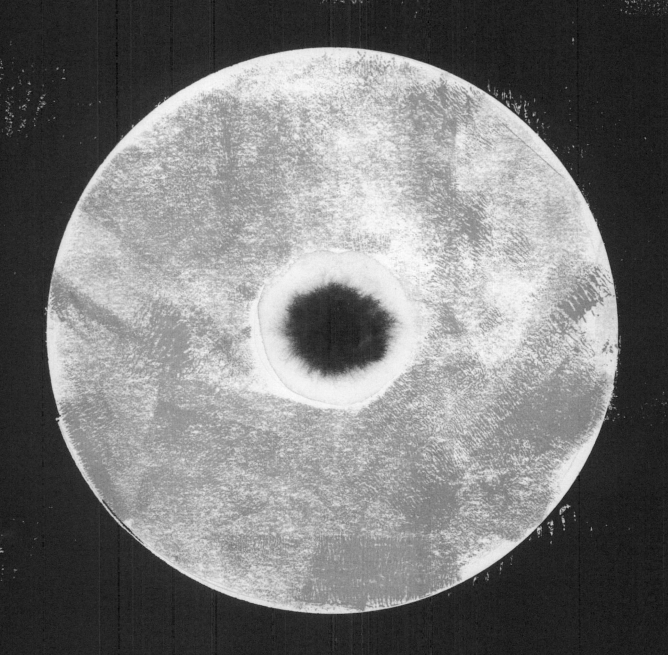

Boobies are great!

THE END
(Butt, that's another book.)

For Lu

Thanking Dr McKevitt for the save, Mai for being rad,
Black Sheep for aftercare, Silver for the dare, Jackie
who dared, and R, AN, AY, RPG for being there.
Remembering Joanne (1963-2018).

"Your breast ... potential."
Susan M. Love, MD, MBA, with Karen Lindsey
and Elizabeth Love. *Dr. Susan Love's Breast Book*, Sixth
Edition (Boston: Da Capo Press, 2015), p. 3. With thanks to
Dr. Susan Love Foundation for Breast Cancer Research.

Sculptures, from left to right: Venus of Willendorf, Austria;
Cycladic sculpture, Greece; Akua'ba doll, Ghana.

Text and illustrations copyright © 2022 by Nancy Vo

Published in 2022 by Groundwood Books / House of Anansi Press
groundwoodbooks.com

We gratefully acknowledge for their financial support of our publishing program the Canada Council for the Arts,
the Ontario Arts Council and the Government of Canada.

Canada Council   Conseil des Arts   ONTARIO ARTS COUNCIL   With the participation of the Government of Canada   Canada
for the Arts   du Canada   CONSEIL DES ARTS DE L'ONTARI   Avec la participation du gouvernement du Canada
                                        an Ontario government agency
                                        un organisme du gouvernement de l'Ontario

Library and Archives Canada Cataloguing in Publication
Title: Boobies / Nancy Vo.
Names: Vo, Nancy, author, illustrator.
Identifiers: Canadiana (print) 20210339721 | Canadiana (ebook) 2021033973X |
ISBN 9781773066929 (hardcover) | ISBN 9781773066936 (EPUB) |
ISBN 9781773066943 (Kindle)
Subjects: LCSH: Breast—Juvenile literature.
Classification: LCC QL944 .V62 2022 | DDC j612.6/64—dc23

The stencil art was made with matte acrylics and pen on paper.
Design by Michael Solomon
Printed and bound in Canada

Your breast is the only organ in your body that you are not born with.
You come into the world with a nipple and lots of potential. — Dr. Susan Love